Origins

Restoring the Identity, Mission, and Leadership of God's Greatest Creation!

Steve Eden

Origins

ISBN: 9781686331220

CHAPTERS

*To the greatest Mom in
the whole wide world!
your love for me made
this book possible!
I love you!
Steve*

DEDICATION

I would like to dedicate this book to my mom, Dot Eden,
who has always shown me the pathway to Christ, taught me
how to war in the Spirit, and cling to the truth. Thank you
Mom! I Love You!

Chapter One
And Now a Word from Your Creator...

The purpose of this book is to infuse identity, mission, and leadership into God's people. How, you ask? God's Word is truth and God's Word is very clear: You are not random, God is not a random God, and He doesn't release truth to us because He is bored.

When God speaks either personally to you or corporately to a group, He does it with the full intention of our receiving what He says, taking it in with confidence, and walking it out in heartfelt obedience and partnership.

Perhaps it is time to consider that it was God's purpose that summoned your existence – let that sink in. The reason you were made manifest, the reason God opened time and inserted you into it - is because He has equipped you with something your generation, your family, and your world needs. You might have come through your parents but you came from God and that makes you significant!

Psalm 139:13-18 says, "For you created my

inmost being; you knit me together in my mother's womb. 14 I praise you because I am fearfully and wonderfully made; your works are wonderful, I know that full well. 15 My frame was not hidden from you when I was made in the secret place, when I was woven together in the depths of the earth. 16 Your eyes saw my unformed body; all the days ordained for me were written in your book before one of them came to be. 17 How precious to me are your thoughts, God! How vast is the sum of them! 18 Were I to count them, they would outnumber the grains of sand— when I awake, I am still with you."

According to this passage, God ordained your days! He knew your end from your beginning before you even arrived on Earth! His thoughts toward you far outnumber all the grains of sand. Yet, we will let the devil tell us we are worthless? We will let the enemy or the voice of others tell us we don't matter?

Let us rise together and say, "NO MORE!"

Let us begin to assign more value to what our Creator/Manufacturer says about us than anyone or anything else, including ourselves!

Take It to the Bank

If you're like me, you get a monthly bank statement of the activity and the balance of your account. Without question I always assign more value to the bank's "account" of what's in my account than my "account" of what's in my account.

When looking at our worth, potential, and value in God's eyes it's the same. We should never assign more value to "our account" of what is in our account than "God's account" of what is in our account! Often our account of what's in our account is based on human feelings, thoughts, behaviors, and everything else that comes at us from the natural world, but God's account of what's in our account is based on the bedrock of Spirit and truth. What joy to find out we have more in there than we thought we did!

The enemy never wants you looking to truth to discover who you really are, what you really have, and what you can do through Christ, your strength! He wants you looking to your feelings, experiences, and reasoning.

We buy into all kinds of psychobabble on TV and media that tells us we are just a random creation that evolved from ancient "cosmic goo," then to "zoo," then to "you." It takes far more faith to believe that, or that a monkey passed its internal moral code to you, than it does to believe a loving Father put you here and gave you a conscience that asks questions such as: "How did I get here?" "Why am I here?" and "Who put me here?"

What if the theory of evolution is propagated to the masses not because the powers that be believe it to be true, but because they know it will keep your children believing they're random, meaningless, and insignificant? If your children believe that, then those powers can make them dependent on them and possibly one day try to enslave them.

Jeremiah 1:5-10 says, "Before I formed you in the womb I knew you; Before you were born I sanctified you; I ordained you a prophet to the nations." 6 Then said I: "Ah, Lord God! Behold, I cannot speak, for I am a youth." 7 But the Lord said to me: "Do not say, 'I am a youth,' For you shall go to all to whom I send you, And whatever I command you, you shall speak. 8 Do

*not be afraid of their faces, For I am with you to
deliver you," says the Lord. 9 Then the Lord put
forth His hand and touched my mouth, and the
Lord said to me: "Behold, I have put My words in
your mouth. 10 See, I have this day set you over
the nations and over the kingdoms, to root out
and to pull down, to destroy and to throw down,
to build and to plant."*

This Scripture says God knew Jeremiah before he
was formed in the womb. It adds God set him
apart and appointed him before he was even born.
God is telling him, "You are significant and I am
going to do big things through you." Jeremiah,
like many of us, didn't believe Him.

*In John 15:16 Jesus adds, "You did not choose
Me, but I chose you and appointed you that you
should go and bear fruit, and that your fruit
should remain, that whatever you ask the Father
in My name He may give you."*

Too many of us believe God has greatness for
others but when it comes to us – not so much.

I am so tired of the doctrines and philosophies of
men robbing us of our mission and our value.
You are so much on God's radar, He completed

you before He began you and I can assure you, as my friend Bruce Barteaux says, "You are not gonna' be God's first failure!"

The Lord gave me this prophetic word for His people in 2015: "I can't have you down or locked into discouragement. For you are My light and salt in this world. My purpose summoned your existence. Would I have made you if you were not carrying something your generation has need of? You are not random. You are not by chance. You are MINE."

Clearly your Creator/Manufacturer, who gave His very life for you in Christ, has destined you for impact and influence. God gave you His Name, His Spirit, His Son, His Word, His Kingdom, and His Love – never let anyone tell you your life doesn't matter!

In Matthew 5:14-16 (MSG) Jesus said, "You're here to be light, bringing out the God-colors in the world. God is not a secret to be kept. We're going public with this, as public as a city on a hill. If I make you light-bearers, you don't think I'm going to hide you under a bucket, do you? I'm putting you on a light stand. Now that I've put you there hilltop, on a light stand—shine!

Keep open house; be generous with your lives. By opening up to others, you'll prompt people to open up with God, this generous Father in heaven."

God didn't light you to hide you! We must continually lay hold of God's truth about us and dare to believe it no matter how good it is. For it is the light of God's goodness and love shining through us that allows people who may not be looking for God to have an encounter with the God who's looking for them.

In 2017, I heard the Lord say to His people, "Strength and might are yours as I am moving you deeper into faith. I am making you more comfortable believing all I say about you. I created you so I could be with you. It's ok to believe it, it was My idea. I redeemed you with My Son's precious blood. It's ok to believe it, it was My idea. I made you righteous and clean. It's ok to believe it, it was My idea. I made you adequate and complete in Me. It's ok to believe that too, it was My idea. When the time was just right, when the world needed your gifts, I opened eternity and formed you in your mother's womb. It's ok to believe all I've done for you, it was ALL My idea."

Get Anchored In Truth!

Be careful what voices you let determine your value, identity, and significance because it is God that determines the vastness of our purpose and potential; no one else. When negative voices or emotions come, ask this question, "Does this line up with who Jesus says I am and what He can do through me?" If it does not, evict it and sever ties with it immediately.

There is nothing more important than the source of your thoughts and ideas about yourself, about God, about truth, and about how life is to be lived. We absolutely can limit God and hinder our impact by how we think, feel, and believe about ourselves.

Your perspective is actually greater than your reality because you will live based on what you perceive to be true, even if it's not! Your belief is actually greater than your behavior because your behavior comes from what you believe. My prayer is that your own beliefs and views of yourself and God are not the greatest hindrance to your purpose and potential being realized.

We should question the source of our thoughts and ideas more. I challenge young people with this a lot. The reason is because not every thought you have (or your teenager has) comes from you, them, or God. There is an enemy who tries to kill, cheat, and deceive all of us. He will take a fleeting feeling or deceptive thought a young person has and tell them, "That's who you are." If they believe him and buy into his lie, pathways to destruction so often follow.

We tend to become who and what we think about ourselves so why not line it up with God's truth? After all, the most humble thing you can do is agree with who God says you are. Humility doesn't mean you never say anything positive about yourself, it means your opinion of you doesn't matter – because it is God's opinion of you that matters.

Isn't it time we acknowledge God knows more about us than we do? Scripture says He has numbered the hairs on our head, yet we have no idea which hair is number 7 or even number 77! God does though! That is proof He knows more about us than we do. Therefore, the wisest thing we could ever do is humble ourselves and agree with who He says we are, what He says we can accomplish, and all He says we possess.

It's hard to believe what God says about us because we've let the world, our feelings, our flesh patterns, and the enemy cause us to think so poorly of ourselves. We live in a blizzard of distraction, technology, information, and deception so it's imperative we anchor ourselves to God's Word and truth instead! God has told me so many times, "Steve, no one else can name you because I've already named you!"

Man's greatest threat, contrary to the news, is not global warming or political unrest, it is ignorance of who we really are, Who made us, and how God designed us to function.

Romans 8:29-31 (TPT) says, "For he knew all about us before we were born and he destined us from the beginning to share the likeness of his Son. This means the Son is the oldest among a vast family of brothers and sisters who will become just like him. 30 Having determined our destiny ahead of time, he called us to himself and transferred his perfect righteousness to everyone he called. And those who possess his perfect righteousness he co-glorified with his Son! 31 So, what does all this mean? If God has determined to stand with us, tell me, who then could ever stand against us?"

God foreknew us, predestined us, gave us His righteousness, called us, and co-glorified us with His Son! Never again will we allow the enemy to tell us we don't matter and move us off our purpose. Never again will we let life and circumstances define us instead of God's truth!

God made you with a purpose and a gifting in mind that you might discover Him, be developed in your intimate knowing of Him, and be deployed as His Kingdom ambassador.
It's time to start believing Him!

<u>Seven Truths to Begin Your Day:</u>

- The truest thing about you is what God says about you.
- Satan knows your name but calls you by your sin. Jesus knows your sin but calls you by your name! (Righteous, Forgiven, Accepted)
- Do NOT let the enemy reduce you to just surviving or hoping someone says something nice so you can feel better about yourself. The only way to consistently feel better about yourself is to KNOW your value in Christ.

- Don't let how people treat you every day be what lifts or lowers you. Understand you didn't wake up to be popular today, you woke up for HIS glory and HIS great Name to be revealed.
- Never let the enemy convince you that you are the way you are because of somebody else's actions or attitudes. That is a victim mindset and powerless.
- Living every day for the acceptance and approval of others is no way to live at all. Instead set your mind on how accepted you are in Christ.
- If you're living each day for people to treat you right, you'll only be doing as good as you're getting treated. Instead, focus on how Jesus treats you each day. If you must live by the motto, "Well, he did it to me first," make sure you're talking about Jesus!

Chapter Two
Origins

Origin means: "The point or place where something begins, arises, or is sourced."

While there are times we must go forward in our journey to find truth, sometimes we must go backward to find it. In this chapter, let us go back to our beginning to discover not only what has been hidden from us but also what has been INTENDED for us!

The late Myles Munroe said, "To know your destination as God's creation, you need to know your beginning. After all, one of the definitions of truth is original information."

Our Beginning

Genesis 1:26-28 says, "Then God said, "Let Us make man in Our image, according to Our likeness; let them have dominion over the fish of the sea, over the birds of the air, and over the cattle, over all the earth and over every creeping thing that creeps on the earth." 27 So God created man in His own image; in the image of

God He created him; male and female He created them. 28 Then God blessed them, and God said to them, "Be fruitful and multiply; fill the earth and subdue it; have dominion over the fish of the sea, over the birds of the air, and over every living thing that moves on the earth."

In reading God's original intent in this passage, it is evident that mankind has lost sight of the manner of life He intended for us. God built us and birthed us to partner with Him in governing the earth. To get back to that, He desires to shift our mindset from thinking like mere church members to thinking like His children, from thinking like mere sheep to thinking like shepherds, and from thinking we are just unclean sinners saved by grace to knowing we are righteous citizens of His Kingdom!

I seriously doubt in the garden Adam and Eve equated their relationship with God to an hour on Sunday. The Bible never says they did what they wanted all week, but then made sure on the weekend they gave God a good hour of their time. So, since Jesus came to restore the relationship mankind lost in the garden of Eden, then He must restore us to what we lost – a day to day, heart to heart, thought to thought, Spirit to spirit united relationship with our Heavenly Father!

Jesus, the Model Son

The Apostle Paul called Jesus the last or second Adam in 1 Corinthians 15:45. I truly believe Jesus came to do and be what the first Adam was created to do and be.

Jesus came as a Master Light illuminating us to our own original plan and design in God. Every single time He said, "Follow Me," He was not only inviting us to back to God but also to live in the truth of our original mission and purpose.

Here's a thought: Jesus Christ said in John 14:6, "I am the way, the **truth**, and the life." I have long believed that He wasn't just saying to us, "I am the way to Heaven…" but also "I am the way you're designed to live, I am the truth about you, and I am the life to be expressed through your body."

If Jesus' daily Spirit led relationship with His Heavenly Father was in part to reveal the truth about us and our original purpose, then we have vastly missed our step and our mission.

Nothing in the Genesis account of mankind's creation suggests God had anything less for us than walking and talking intimately with Him each day. Just like Jesus, from a close and intimate relationship, we would represent our Father and reproduce His image throughout the physical realm called Earth — walking among humanity and doing them good.

I honestly believe God created the Earth for the purpose of colonizing it with His children, governing it by His Spirit, and filling it with Heaven's glory! This was Jesus' mission. He even introduced a prayer that detailed the assignment: "Our Father Who art in Heaven, hallowed be Thy Name, Thy Kingdom come, Thy will be done, *on earth as it is in Heaven.*"

It seems so simple. Historian and Author H.G. Wells, upon reading the New Testament stated, "This is the greatest proposition ever introduced to mankind. Jesus desired to change the culture of the Earth to look like Heaven." Jesus was revealing our original dominion mandate by showing us what God created us to do.

Unfortunately, the focus of the modern church has been to get everyone off the planet and into Heaven, thus blinding us from our mission and God-given purpose. I grew up thinking my faith was for getting to Heaven instead of to extend all of Heaven's influence on Earth. It was not until a few years ago I realized, "No one in Heaven needs my help, they're all here!"

People ask me why I don't preach more on the second coming of Jesus, and I simply say, "Because we haven't really discovered the gospel of His first coming yet. We have such little understanding of Jesus' mission that restored our identity, dominion, and leadership in the Earth!"

Perhaps it's time to ditch the idea we are all here just to "hang on 'til Heaven" and realize we are here to reveal our Father's great Name! Jesus modeled this as *our* way, *our* truth, and *our* life.

Overcoming Religious Identities

Nowhere in the Genesis account of our creation does it say God offered man religion. Nowhere does it record God said, "Let's create a bunch of religions but let them all lead to Me."

Jesus didn't come to start a religion, He came to restore a relationship!!

Jesus isn't even a religious figure! He is NOT to be laid alongside Buddha, Muhammad, or Confucius, as if He competes with them for religious followers! Jesus Christ is a King! He is THE KING of the universe, the Maker of all, not some religious icon we pay homage to!

Jesus is different in that He puts His Spirit inside our heart not just His values and principles in our head. Life in, by, and through His Spirit will always trump religious morality because it comes with God's actual life, power, and poise.

Religion is so crippling because it makes us identify ourselves as members of a religious organization instead of Christ filled sons and daughters who are powerful citizens of our Father's Kingdom.

I have nothing against church membership but nowhere in Scripture are we instructed to "identify" ourselves as members of a religious organization. God never even called us Christians; pagans called us that. God calls us citizens and sons! Citizens of the Kingdom

(Ephesians 2:19) and children of God (John 1:12) have rights and privileges, whereas religious people have obligations. One is empowering, one is powerless.

Instead of seeing ourselves as God's offspring and partners in extending His love throughout the Earth, we tend to work independently of Him, stuck in our own resources, dreaming about going to Heaven when we die. We fail to grasp Jesus' clear mission which was far more focused on getting what was in Heaven into Earth than getting what was in Earth into Heaven. On more than one occasion He announced, "Repent, for the Kingdom of Heaven is at hand."

In religion, man works to appease his deity's demands, but in God's Kingdom the King supplies His delegates all His resource in partnership. In religion, man is taught to earn "blessing" via self-effort, but in God's Kingdom we use the inner resources of Jesus Christ our Vine to take dominion and influence this world with God's goodness. We can either live like we are earning something from God (religion) or we can live knowing we already have something (Kingdom citizen). We can either live FOR Christ or FROM Christ.

As new creations in Christ, we not only have our Supply from Christ, we are freed from the religious bondage of "rule-keeping." Instead of being outwardly restrained, we have been inwardly transformed! The old sin nature has given way to the new nature of Christ's Spirit that wants to live holy.

Bob Yandian wrote in his study on the book of Galatians, "If God's new creation children cannot be set free to live, speak, love, and be led by the Holy Spirit; but must be chained by a reward system of do's and don'ts, then the new birth is no better or more powerful than the old life of sin. If that's true God simply took us out of one bondage into another. Grace is not a license to sin, but a license to serve. Grace sets us free not to do wrong but to do what our new creation heart wants to do! In the end, Father God has given us actual freedom to serve Him and binds us with something far greater than do's and don'ts - His internal presence and love. This, friends, is why Jesus came!"

Scripture says in Romans 8:14-17 (TPT), "The mature children of God are those who are moved by the impulses of the Holy Spirit. 15 And you did not receive the "spirit of religious duty," leading you back into the fear of never being good enough. But you have received the "Spirit of full acceptance," enfolding you into the family of God. And you will never feel orphaned, for as he rises up within us, our spirits join him in saying the words of tender affection, "Beloved Father!" 16 For the Holy Spirit makes God's fatherhood real to us as he whispers into our innermost being, "You are God's beloved child!" 17 And since we are his true children, we qualify to share all his treasures, for indeed, we are heirs of God himself. And since we are joined to Christ, we also inherit all that he is and all that he has."

This passage is full of marvelous revelation! In Christ, we are God's fully accepted, beloved, and Spirit-filled children, as well as joint heirs with Jesus! In other words, all He inherited from His Father, you received when He came inside you to live! He called God "Father" so you could call God "Father." He took dominion for His Father's Kingdom so you could take dominion for your Father's Kingdom. The best way to honor Him is to recognize He shared all He has with you so you too can live as a citizen and son. We do not glorify Jesus when our mindset is, "He got it all, but we have nothing."

Jesus lived a day to day, heart to heart, thought to thought, Spirit to Spirit, united and intimate relationship with His Father. That is clearly from our origin what God intended for all of us as well. Get born again, get filled with the Holy Spirit and get after it!

<u>Six Directives from Jesus to His Church:</u>

- Shift your focus from going to Heaven to filling the Earth with the glory of God.
- Shift your focus from fatalism and escapism to victorious Spirit led living.
- Shift your focus from identifying as church members to identifying as citizens of Christ's Kingdom.
- Shift your focus from stockpiling members to sending leaders.
- Shift your focus from preparing God's people to *leave* the planet to preparing God's people to *lead* the planet.
- Shift your focus from separated congregations and denominations to the united body of Christ. Churches should be partnering together to bring Godly transformation to their towns and cities.

Chapter Three
The Restoration of What Was Lost

If the results of the fall of Adam in Genesis chapter three weren't enough to plunge mankind into mass confusion about his identity and his mission; a steady stream of man-made religion compounded the problem. Thank God help came in Jesus Christ the Messiah!

Jesus, Our Hero!

When Adam and Eve "fell" from their position and partnership with God (dragging all future human beings down with them), is there really any way we could get our own selves back up to that position? Of course not! So, Jesus basically says; Father, I will get your children back for you. I will restore not only their ability to see Your image in themselves, but I will make it so You can again see Your image in them. This is one of the most loving things Jesus did – making it possible for Father God to see Himself in His most precious creation once again.

Jesus understood God could only see Himself in us again if His Spirit was returned to reside in us as it was in the beginning. How could God see His own "Holiness" within His children unless His "Holy" Spirit was present!

Recognizing our need for God's Spirit and internal presence, Jesus chose to come to the Earth to "*restore*" what we lost. To "restore" according to Webster's dictionary means to place something "back" in its original position and condition! Yet, performance based religion has taught us we can never experience with God what we once had.

Religion at best says we have been partially restored to some kind of a "sinner saved by grace" status. It's like we were at a ten with God before the fall, but even after Jesus came and conquered, He only got us back to about a five. That is not the true definition of "restore!"

This harmful and yet predominant mindset is keenly and profoundly revealed by Jesus in Luke 15 with the parable of the prodigal son.

Luke 15:11-24 says, "Then Jesus said: "A certain man had two sons. 12 And the younger of them said to his father, 'Father, give me the portion of goods that falls to me.' So he divided to them his livelihood. 13 And not many days after, the younger son gathered all together, journeyed to a far country, and there wasted his possessions with prodigal living. 14 But when he had spent all, there arose a severe famine in that land, and he began to be in want. 15 Then he went and joined himself to a citizen of that country, and he sent him into his fields to feed swine. 16 And he would gladly have filled his stomach with the pods that the swine ate, and no one gave him anything. 17 "But when he came to himself, he said, 'How many of my father's hired servants have bread enough and to spare, and I perish with hunger! 18 I will arise and go to my father, and will say to him, "Father, I have sinned against heaven and before you, 19 and I am no longer worthy to be called your son. Make me like one of your hired servants."' 20 "And he arose and came to his father. But when he was still a great way off, his father saw him and had compassion, and ran and fell on his neck and kissed him. 21 And the son said to him, 'Father, I have sinned against heaven and in your sight, and am no longer worthy to be called your son.' 22 "But the father said to his servants, 'Bring out the best robe and put it on him, and put a ring on his hand and sandals on his feet. 23 And bring the fatted calf here and kill it, and let us eat and

*be merry; 24 for this my son was dead and is
alive again; he was lost and is found.' And they
began to be merry."*

Notice after the prodigal son came to himself, he
undervalues his father's goodness and love so
much he requests to be a slave when he returns.
In other words, he's going to ask his father to live
in the bunkhouse with other slaves, so he can
keep his relationship at a distance, figuring he
could never have back what he had lost.

I love his father's reaction! Instead of agreeing
with the boy, He initiates total restoration of
sonship! First, the father runs and tackles his son,
then he brings out his robe, ring, and sandals.
This is a major action on the father's part because
that signet ring literally means his son has
authority once again to act on his father's behalf
and to represent him! I pray you see the absolute
parallels between the prodigal's father and your
Heavenly Father!

In John 1:12 it says when we receive Christ we
have the "right" (power or privilege) to be God's
children! The word "right" according to the
Strong's Concordance, includes power to act on
our Father's behalf! From our origin, this

representation is exactly what God had in mind for us! In Genesis chapter one we were created, told Whose image we were made in, and then given authority by God to act on His behalf here on Earth.

Jesus, in telling this parable, is exposing the religious mentality of separation and defeatism that we could never have back what we lost because we are "unclean sinners." It's rooted in performance-based identity which says, "If I do bad, then I am bad." Your behavior never determines the truth about you! What God has done in you at your new birth is your true identity.

2 Corinthians 5:17 says, "If any man is in Christ he is a new creation, old things have passed away, all things have become new."

By definition of a "new creation," I cannot be what and who I used to be! God's power that recreated me now determines my real identity, not my performance.

If you'll start believing, seeing, and thinking correctly, you'll start living correctly. Religion is always trying to modify your behavior while God is trying to get you to believe what He has done inside you!

Jesus also reveals in the prodigal parable the true gospel that He came to "*restore*" our original spiritual position and sonship with our Heavenly Father! I assure you Jesus did not come to relegate us to an "I'm just an "unclean sinner" mentality!"

It seems, like the prodigal son, we as the people of God have failed to realize the **restoring**, **re-deeming**, and **reconciling** power of Jesus Christ to take us BACK to our original position and condition with God before the fall. Too often we have assigned more faith and value to our mistakes than His ability to cleanse us.

The Prefix "Re"

"Re" is a prefix that means again, to go back, or to return. "Re" is used in all the following New Testament words:

- Restore – To put something back in its original position, condition, or form.

- Redeem – To buy back. To release or set free by paying a full ransom. To restore something back to the possession of its rightful owner. To rescue from the power and possession of a foreign or illegitimate owner.

- Reconcile – To make one, to bring into harmony or agreement.

- Receive – To come into possession of, to acquire, to take back.

- Repent – To change your mind and realign with higher thinking. ("Pent" is where we get the word penthouse. If you join it to the prefix "re" then it's an instruction for us to go back to thinking on a higher level.)

If my English classes in school served me well; then the above words, because of the "re" prefix, imply that Jesus Christ came to take us back to what we once had! Even in John 20:22 when Jesus "*breathed*" on His disciples and said, "*receive* the Holy Spirit," this implies the disciples were taking back a Spirit we had possessed before which is the literal definition and origin of the word receive.

Not only did Jesus come to restore the relationship we lost with God in the garden of Eden, it appears He symbolically initiated it by breathing on His disciples which is what God did at our creation!

Genesis 2:7 (NASB) says, "Then the LORD God formed man of the dust from the ground, and <u>breathed into his nostrils the breath of life</u>; and man became a living being."

Jesus came to restore us as: The righteousness of God, children of God, citizens and ambassadors of His Kingdom, joint heirs, partakers of God's divine nature, ministers of the new covenant, priests and kings, and the light of the world.

Notice all of those have to do with our role here on Earth not in Heaven. Why? We didn't fall from Heaven, Lucifer did! We fell from our leadership position in the Earth. We must lose our escapism mindset and recapture our victory in Jesus mindset! It bears repeating, we didn't fall from a Sunday morning relationship with God either! We fell from a day to day, Spirit to spirit, heart to heart relationship with our Father and Creator!

Contrasting Christ and Adam

The magnitude of Christ's restoration work is all here in Romans 5:15-19 (TPT) "15 Now, there is no comparison between Adam's transgression and the gracious gift that we experience. For the magnitude of the gift (Christ gave) far outweighs the crime."

Why would we assign more value to Adam's ability to make us wrong than Jesus' ability to make us right? What Paul is describing here would be like Jesus walking into the courtroom of God to pay the fine for Adam's sin, throwing a gold brick down on the desk and saying, "This should more than do it!" And it did!

Verse 15 continues with the comparison…

"It's true that many died because of one man's transgression, but how much greater will God's grace and his gracious gift of acceptance overflow to many because of what one Man, Jesus, the Messiah, did for us! 16 And this free-flowing gift imparts to us much more than what was given to us through the one who sinned. For because of one transgression, we are all facing a death sentence with a verdict of "Guilty!" But this gracious gift leaves us free from our many

failures and brings us into the perfect righteousness of God—acquitted with the words "Not guilty!" 17 Death once held us in its grip, and by the blunder of one man (Adam), death reigned as king over humanity. But now, how much more are we held in the grip of grace and continue reigning as kings in life, enjoying our regal freedom through the gift of perfect righteousness in the one and only Jesus, the Messiah! 18 In other words, just as condemnation came upon all people through one transgression, so through one righteous act of Jesus' sacrifice, the perfect righteousness that makes us right with God and leads us to a victorious life is now available to all. 19 One man's disobedience opened the door for all humanity to become sinners. So also one man's obedience opened the door for many to be made perfectly right with God and acceptable to him."

If you look at Romans 5:17, it says death reigned in the Earth since the fall of Adam, but because of what Jesus made available to us, it says we can REIGN again as kings in life. In other words, our dominion mandate from Genesis 1 returned to us when Jesus made it possible for the Spirit of God to return to us.

While I understand the world and much of creation is still subject to the fall of man, those of us in Christ are new creations in Him! We are not just old sinners. We are righteous, redeemed children in our spirits and once again possessors of our Heavenly Father's DNA.

Because you have been born again, two wonderful things happened! You got born out of "The Adam's Family" and you got born into "The Family of God!" Duane Sheriff shares a great comparison of everything you need to know about who you used to be in Adam and who you are now in Christ!!

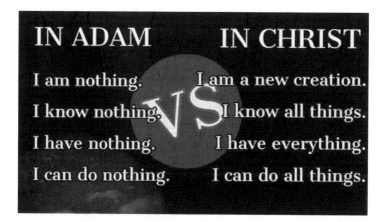

You've Been Sealed!

In John 6:27 Jesus said the Father had set His

"seal" upon Him. I believe this happened in Luke 3:21-22 when Jesus comes up from His own water baptism, the Heavens open, the Holy Spirit alights upon Him in the form of a dove, and God declares, "You are My beloved Son, in you I am well pleased." The Holy Spirit in and upon Jesus was proof He had come from God and He was His Father's Son. The Holy Spirit is also how He was able to go about "doing good and healing all who were oppressed of the devil" as Acts 10:38 states.

In 2 Corinthians 1:21-22 and Ephesians 1:13 the Bible says you and I have been "sealed" with the same Holy Spirit of promise. According to the Strong's Concordance, these are the same Greek words for "seal" as appeared in John 6:27 with Jesus. It connotes not only ownership, but also that He has given you a signet ring which allows a child to represent their father! This seal attests to a father's authority and validation!

2 Corinthians 1:21-22 says, "Now He who establishes us with you in Christ and has anointed us is God, 22 who also has sealed us and given us the Spirit in our hearts as a guarantee."

Ephesians 1:13 says, "In Him you also trusted, after you heard the word of truth, the gospel of your salvation; in whom also, having believed, <u>you were sealed with the Holy Spirit of promise</u>... "

When you look at the restoration work of Christ, as well as you being sealed, validated, and accepted via God's Holy Spirit, there's only one conclusion: God put you here to know Him and make Him known and crush every gate hell throws up in front of you.

As Francis Chan stated, "We ought to be able to drop any Christian off in any city in the world and they should effectively grow in Jesus, walk with the Holy Spirit, make disciples, establish spiritual family, and carry on the mission of Jesus."

Five Points to Remember:

- Jesus restored you ALL the way back to your Father not just half way back.
- By definition of a new creation, you are not who you used to be.
- For all Adam's sin did to you, the grace of Jesus Christ is far greater.

- You have been given authority to act on your Father's behalf.
- The Holy Spirit is God's seal of approval in and upon you.

Chapter Four
Hello, Holy Spirit!!!

Jesus was the most important person on Earth, not just because of what He said and did, but because of what He made available again to us – Life in and through God's Spirit. The Holy Spirit is not some impersonal, random influence. He is a person divine with Whom we can commune, from Whom we can draw resources, and Who needs to be the Life of our life. He is also the One who delivers and executively produces God's Kingdom on Earth.

The Lord told me once, "Steve, if you know how the Kingdom of God *came*, then you can understand how it *still comes today*." Here are a few of the passages He showed me:

In Matthew 12:28, Jesus says, "If I drive out demons <u>by the Spirit of God, the Kingdom of God comes.</u>"

Romans 14:17 adds, "<u>The Kingdom of God is</u> not eating and drinking, but righteousness, peace, and joy <u>in the Holy Spirit.</u>"

1 Corinthians 4:20 says, "<u>The Kingdom of God is</u>

not in word but in power."

In Mark 9:1 Jesus says, "Assuredly, I say to you that there are some standing here who will not taste death till they see the kingdom of God PRESENT with power."

In Acts 1:8 Jesus says, "And you shall receive power when the Holy Spirit comes upon you..."

Acts 10:38 records, "God anointed Jesus of Nazareth with the Holy Spirit and power, and He went about doing good and healing all who were oppressed of the devil."

In each of these four passages, the word "power" is translated from the Greek word dunamis which means "miraculous power; power via God's ability."

Even in Luke 1:30-38, the power of the Holy Spirit is central in the very King Of Heaven's entrance into the Earth's physical realm. After Mary asks the angel Gabriel a very legitimate question about how God's Son and His Kingdom will manifest, Gabriel said to Mary, **"The Holy Spirit will come..."** and **"The *power* of the highest will overshadow you..."**

Once again here in Luke chapter one, the word "power" is translated from the Greek word dunamis.

If it took the Holy Spirit to manifest the King of Heaven in the Earth back then, I am sure it takes the Holy Spirit to manifest the Kingdom of Heaven in the Earth today.

According to Jesus and the above passages, I am absolutely convinced:

- The Kingdom of God is in the Holy Spirit and more specifically the dunamis power of the Holy Spirit.
- It is by the Spirit of God the Kingdom of God comes.
- The dominion of Heaven still comes in and through the dunamis power of the Holy Spirit today.

Maybe you were taught God's Kingdom is solely a future event. Perhaps you're waiting on God's Kingdom to come, or like me, you believe it has come *in part* through the Holy Spirit but won't be present in its fullness until the second coming of Christ.

Hopefully, we can all agree that throughout history there are ample examples of God's Kingdom breaking through into the physical realm in power:

- The miraculous birth of Jesus Christ
- The resurrection of Jesus Christ
- The liberation of the Gadarene demoniac
- The resurrection of Lazarus
- The healing of the man born blind
- The coming of the Holy Spirit in the upper room filling the disciples
- The healing of the man at the gate beautiful through Peter and John
- The seventy disciples returning with great joy saying, "Lord, even the demons are subject to us in Your Name"
- Daniel in the lion's den
- The 3 Hebrew boys in the fiery furnace
- The parting of the Red Sea
- Jesus healing lepers by touching them
- Jesus and the disciples feeding the 5,000
- All those born again, filled, healed, sealed, taught, empowered, and delivered by the Spirit of God today!

The Cross Was the Means to the Spirit

While the Bible is a book about redemption, it's a book about something larger than redemption. While the Bible is a book about salvation and healing, it's about something larger than salvation and healing. The Bible is a book about the Supreme Ruler, the ruled, and the realm from which He rules.

Jesus' mission was to reintroduce God's Kingdom *to us*, by putting God's Spirit back *in us*, so He could advance God's Kingdom *through us*.

Jesus mentioned the word church three times, all in Matthew; but He mentioned the word Kingdom over 100 times! This is not to say the church is unimportant; it is. Jesus loves the church and birthed it in the power of the Holy Spirit as recorded in the book of Acts. I do believe however, that this does reveal the church wasn't His central focus. Clearly that distinction belongs to the Kingdom of God.

This is why Jesus never said, "Make sure you get saved, water baptized, join a church, and when you're dead you can go to Heaven." Instead, He routinely preached and asked His disciples to preach, "The Kingdom of God is at hand," while demonstrating its arrival via the power of the Spirit. Adam's fall took God's Spirit, intimacy, and Kingdom mandate out of our reach, but Jesus made it accessible again!

I love the blood of Jesus, and I'm so eternally thankful for the cross. I glory in His resurrection and His triumph over death, hell, and the grave. But all of those were simply a means to His end goal – restoring our sonship and partnership with God by the gift of the Holy Spirit! There is no way God intended Adam and Eve to just be second class citizens and roll with whatever life on Earth dealt them. He told them to take dominion and extend His image throughout the Earth, but the return of the Spirit was needed.

The cross where Jesus absorbed and became our sin and shed His innocent blood was "necessary" for the Spirit of God to be able to live in us again. Only then could we properly represent our Heavenly Father as He always intended.

God's original instruction to take dominion (Genesis 1:26-28), returned when His Spirit returned -- first in Jesus, then in us! All four gospels, plus Acts chapter one, record that John the Baptist baptized with water unto repentance, but Jesus Christ would baptize and immerse us in the Holy Spirit! This was a major part of Jesus' assignment because no one can be like God without God! No one can extend His presence, person, and power without Him.

Jesus didn't cleanse you to leave you empty! If we take Jesus' life, death, and resurrection but don't take the gift of the Holy Spirit, we will have an impersonal and powerless gospel that lives *in history* but not *in us!*

E. Stanley Jones summed it up when he said, "Jesus lived, died, rose again, AND NOW lives in us through the gift of the Holy Spirit. To take the first three, but stop short of the fourth is the supreme tragedy of modern Christianity."

Leaving Only After the Job Is Done

I can assure you Jesus was not about to leave this planet until His assignment was complete. Therefore, a great question to ask is, "When did Jesus actually leave?"

He didn't leave after He shed His blood. He

didn't leave after the cross. He didn't even leave after He rose again. We find Him all the way into Acts chapter one, after His resurrection, teaching His disciples about the Kingdom of God; not the importance of church attendance, nor the priority of church growth. He's preparing them for the Spirit of dominion to be *restored* in fullness.

Acts 1:1-9 says, "The former account I made, O Theophilus, of all that Jesus began both to do and teach, 2 until the day in which He was taken up, after He through the Holy Spirit had given commandments to the apostles whom He had chosen, 3 to whom He also presented Himself alive after His suffering by many infallible proofs, <u>being seen by them during forty days and</u> <u>speaking of the things pertaining to the kingdom</u> <u>of God</u>. 4 And being assembled together with them, He commanded them not to depart from Jerusalem, but to wait for the Promise of the Father, "which," He said, "you have heard from Me; 5 for John truly baptized with water, but you shall be baptized with the Holy Spirit not many days from now." 6 Therefore, when they had come together, they asked Him, saying, "Lord, will You at this time restore the kingdom to Israel?" 7 And He said to them, "It is not for you to know times or seasons which the Father has *put in His own authority. 8 <u>But you shall receive power when the Holy Spirit has come upon you; and you shall be witnesses to Me in Jerusalem, and in all Judea and Samaria, and to the end of the earth.</u>" 9 <u>Now when He had spoken these things, while they watched, He was taken up, and a cloud received Him out of their sight.</u>"*

Only after He says, "You shall receive power when the Holy Spirit comes upon you…" does Jesus then depart. Why? Because now His assignment was complete! He had done all that was necessary to undo the mess the first Adam created by bringing the Holy Spirit back to humanity. As Jesus said in Matthew 12:28, "By the Spirit of God, the Kingdom of God comes." It came, and it came in power, just as He had declared in Mark 9:1!

This return of God's Kingdom via the Spirit was prophesied all over the Old Testament!

- Isaiah 9:6-7 declares "For unto us a child is born, unto us a Son is given, and the government will be upon His shoulder. Of the increase of His government and peace there will be no end."

- Daniel 2:44-45 says the God of Heaven would, "Set up a Kingdom that would never be destroyed."
- Joel 2:28-29 says that in the last days God would, "pour out His Spirit on all flesh."

Perhaps the greatest prophetic picture of God's restoration plan and the coming of His Kingdom via the Holy Spirit though is in Ezekiel 36!

Ezekiel 36:22-27 (NIV) says, "Therefore say to the Israelites, 'This is what the Sovereign LORD says: It is not for your sake, that I am going to do these things, but for the sake of my holy name, which you have profaned among the nations where you have gone. 23 I will show the holiness of my great name, which has been profaned among the nations, the name you have profaned among them. <u>Then the nations will know that I am the LORD, when I am proved holy through you before their eyes.</u> 24 "'For I will take you out of the nations; I will gather you from all the countries and bring you back into your own land. 25 I will sprinkle clean water on you, and you will be clean; <u>I will cleanse you from all your impurities and from all your idols. 26 I will give you a new heart and put a new spirit in you;</u> I will remove from you your heart of stone and give you

*a heart of flesh. 27 And <u>I will put my Spirit in you</u>
and move you to follow my decrees and be
careful to keep my laws."*

We see God is badly misrepresented all over the
planet; and why wouldn't He be since no human
had His Spirit inside! He needed a solution and
oh what a solution it is! "I will put My Spirit
back inside you and reveal My holiness
THROUGH YOU!"

The Journey of the Holy Spirit

The Father's love was the divine intention. The
Son's descent was the divine invasion. The
Spirit's coming was the divine indwelling. God
kept moving closer until He lands in the ultimate
place – within us. Authority and intimacy
became ever so authoritative and intimate when
He moved inside.

After we sinned by declaring our independence
from God in Genesis chapter three, the
government of Heaven took back the Holy Spirit
(the executive producer of God's dominion on
Earth). We had tainted God's dwelling place
(us), and He is a holy God and would not dwell in
an unholy temple.

I believe Heaven's recall of the Spirit is similar to when a nation declares its independence from an occupying country so the occupying country recalls it's governor or representative from that nation. The recalling of the Holy Spirit didn't mean God didn't love us, it just meant we weren't able to represent Him any longer in our fallen condition. Without the Holy Spirit, God's Kingdom could not happen on the Earth.

In the Old Testament, the Holy Spirit took up temporary residence in the tabernacle, temple, and arc of the covenant because God loved us so much He still desired to be among us. The Holy Spirit would also show up and break through in "pinches and sprinkles," but He would never remain or move inside us. He would come upon Samson for an assignment of supernatural strength, but then depart. Samson was not born again because the Spirit never came to stay and never moved inside. This is why the Holy Spirit could not return fully until Jesus shed His blood and cleansed God's original temple (us).

Mankind without the indwelling Spirit is void of power and anointing and is relegated to being religious pretenders (hypocrites) as Jesus called

the Pharisees in Matthew chapter 23. It's similar
to 2 Timothy 3:5 which says in the last days, men
would hold to a form of Godliness but deny its
power. The word 'power' here in the Greek is
dunamis once again.

People can join a church, read the Bible, and even
act like they have authority but without the Spirit,
God is not operating and thus there is a "form" of
Godliness but no real power.

Why Jesus Actually Came:

- To die our death and execute the legitimate
  punishment for our sin.
- To end our independence from God and re-
  establish our dependence on God.
- To cleanse God's original temple (mankind)
  so we could "receive" Christ via the Holy
  Spirit.
- To make inward intimacy between man and
  God possible again.
- To restore our day to day, Spirit to Spirit,
  heart to heart relationship with God.
- To deliver the Governor back to the Earth;
  restoring our identity, dominion, and
  leadership role.

- To restore our Father's Kingdom rule which is in the Holy Spirit.
- To prove His victory over sin and death. The wages of sin is death, therefore to defeat death, the result of sin, is to prove that sin is defeated. He set us free!
- To collect our sin and end it once and for all. Jesus had no sin so He couldn't die. The only way He could die was to take our sin into His body, which He did on the cross.

Chapter Five
The Law of Origination

Genesis 1:1 says, "In the beginning, God created the heavens and the earth."

In the beginning, God created two separate worlds to work together: The heavens and the Earth. One world is seen, and one is unseen. One world is physical, and one is spiritual. One you can hold with your hand, and one you must hold with your heart.

God's plan in creating these two worlds was to take of the one world (Heaven) and put it in the other world (Earth). He would rule the "seen world" from the "unseen world" by living in the "unseen" part of a "seen" creation who is "on the scene" for Him! In other words, God desired to put *His* unseen Spirit inside *your* unseen spirit while giving you a physical body to house Him. I believe He did this so we could together fill the newly created physical Earth with His righteousness, peace, and joy.

In order to carry out this astonishing vision, He designed us perfectly. A creation that is able to access Heaven and touch the Earth!

We Came from God!

God in creating everything, decided first what He needed, then why He needed it, how it would work, and what it would be made out of. When He wanted fish, He spoke to the waters to bring forth fish. When He wanted vegetation, He spoke to the soil to bring forth vegetation. When He wanted stars, He spoke to the firmament to bring forth stars, but when He wanted you, He spoke to Himself! He said, "Let US make man in OUR own image…"

By the law of creation, what is in the water is in the fish. What is in the soil is in the vegetation. What is in the firmament is in the stars; and what is in God is in you! This makes you stunningly significant, incredibly valuable, and filled with God given, God driven, potential!

By the law of origination, every created thing must **abide** (live, remain, stay) in the dimension that sourced and originated it!

Therefore, fish must *abide* in water because fish originated from water and water is life to fish.

Plants must *abide* in soil because plants originated from soil and soil is life to plants. The stars must *abide* in firmament because stars originated from firmament and firmament is life to stars. Finally, man must *abide* in God's Spirit because man originated from God's Spirit and God's Spirit is life to mankind.

In John 6:63, Jesus said, "My words are Spirit and life."

In Romans 8:6 Paul adds, "The mind set on the flesh is death, but the mind set on the Spirit is life and peace."

How can it be that Jesus' Spirit and words are life and peace to us? Because we were created to live by the Spirit by our Creator's intentional, intelligent design!

Galatians 5:25 says, "Since we've been made alive by the Spirit, let us walk by the Spirit."

This is clearly the law of origination. I realize we fell in the garden and were no longer able to abide in God's Spirit, but that's why Jesus Christ came! He came to bring us access to our life source again! In John 10:10 He says, "I came that you might have life and have it more abundantly." He came restoring the Spirit -- the Vine and dimension we were made to abide in. We have full access to our Father again via the new birth and the baptism of the Holy Spirit!

Romans 8:14 says, "For those who are led by the Spirit of God, these are the children of God."

The Christian life in its purest form -- not the man made, watered down religious version -- is undeniably tied to Spirit-sourced living. It is a daily identifying with and knowing of the things of the Spirit. Jesus was conceived in Mary's womb by the Spirit. Jesus was empowered for ministry by the Spirit. Jesus cast out devils by the Spirit. The Church was birthed in Acts by the Spirit. We are born again by the Spirit. We are changed from glory to glory by the Spirit. We are endued with power from on high by the Spirit. We can only understand what God says by the Spirit. We bear fruit by the Spirit. We worship in spirit. God Himself is Spirit.

Using scripture after scripture, I can prove to you the reason for the coming of Jesus Christ was the return of the Spirit of God, man's true Source he originated from.

According to Its Kind

Ten times in Genesis chapter one God uses the phrase, "according to its kind."

Let's pick it up in Genesis 1:24-26: "Then God said, "Let the earth bring forth the living creature according to its kind: cattle and creeping thing and beast of the earth, each according to its kind"; and it was so. 25 And God made the beast of the earth according to its kind, cattle according to its kind, and everything that creeps on the earth according to its kind. And God saw that it was good. 26 Then God said, "Let Us make man in Our image, according to Our likeness..."

Clearly there is a pattern in creation, but only man is fashioned in the likeness or image of God (according to His kind...) This is why we are all predestined to be conformed to the image of God's Son! We were made to like what He likes; love what He loves, and even oppose what He opposes. We will never be able to change this about ourselves because we didn't make ourselves.

Therefore, as I alluded to earlier, God will always

be life and peace to us and sin will always bring disharmony and death. People assume the devil introduced death in Scripture but actually God did. He said, "If you eat of that tree, you will surely die." Death, however, was never made as a "threat" in the garden of Eden. God didn't say, "I'll kill you if you eat of that tree." He simply said death would be the result if we chose to abide in something other than the dimension that originated and sources us - His Spirit. No one has to threaten a fish out of water with death, death is inevitable.

Choosing life outside of God's Spirit is called sin. Sin in the New Testament is defined as "missing the mark" which is the Greek word "hamartia." Missing the mark of what? The only image we were ever created to bear.

In Matthew 22:21, Jesus says something so profound, "Whatever has Caesar's image on it must be rendered back to Caesar but whatever has God's image on it must be rendered back to God." This is no religious philosophy, this is reality. This is why when we sin, we feel less than our true selves.

People think Christianity is a religion,

philosophy, or idealism. No, it's reality! The Creator came here in the person of His Son, telling and showing us how life is to be lived.

Three times the Bible says Jesus, "Taught as One with great authority." This literally means He taught according to the nature of reality.

I've been on this planet 49 years and I've discovered because of our origin, Christ-likeness is not just imperative to a Christian's life but to every human! Our bodies, in all of our incredible design are made by a moral God for morality. Your body is never "neutral" in how it feels about you choosing love over hate or forgiveness over festering bitterness. One is health for your body, the other is not.

1 Corinthians 6:13 says, "The body is for the Lord and the Lord is for the body."

You could add — our heart is for the Lord, our mind is for the Lord, and our spirit is for the Lord. Even an atheist cannot deny the human body, soul, and spirit is at home in love, joy, and peace. On the other hand, our body, heart, and soul break down in prolonged hate, bitterness, or ill will.

If Christ-likeness is written into the mission of our making, the fiber of our being, and the way we are made to live, then sin would not only be wrong for us but also unfulfilling and unhealthy. When people do the right thing, they feel heightened and free because their bodies and minds have an inward bent toward goodness. Our bodies are not neutral about life and our choices, they are made for morality.

One of the things I love about God is He opposes every step of our self-harm. Whether it is lying, fornicating, or unforgiveness; God loves us too much to let us settle down into our lower selves. One Sunday a gentleman came up to me after service and said, "Brother Steve, I feel so free!" I asked him, "What's going on?" He excitedly told me how the Lord had walked him through forgiving a coworker that morning! Notice he was free in forgiveness; not bound in it. He was free in Christ-likeness; not bound in it. He was free in being conformed to God's image; not bound in it.

I read not long ago about a famous atheist blogger. A graduate of Yale university, she started wondering why she felt an inward payoff when she did good for others and tried to help them. She also began to wonder why when she lived solely for her own interests, she found frustration and strained relationships. She began to pursue truth and realized that morality must be objective, not subjective. She said truth is something we humans discover not something we determine. She began to realize morality must be written into us by a Creator (God). She has since joined a local church as she continues her pursuit of more truth and laws of morality at work in her members.

Because You Originated from God's Spirit:

- You are too great a creation to be satisfied by anything but the Spirit of God!
- God has cornered the market on your fulfillment.
- Sin will bring you self-defeat and frustration because God's image and likeness is fashioned in and upon you.
- Sin is unfulfilling, unsatisfying, and unhealthy.
- People who say God doesn't care if you sin don't understand God's love. He protests every step of your self-harm and always will.

- You are eternally at home abiding in God's Spirit, and when you do, you walk the Earth free!
- Your body, mind, and emotions are not neutral, they are made by a moral God for moral living.

Chapter Six
Image and Identity Precede Dominion

For God so loved humanity He gave us His Son.
For the Son so loved humanity He gave us the
Holy Spirit. For the Holy Spirit so loved
humanity He gave us our dominion back!

Genesis 1:26-28 says, "Then God said, "Let Us
make man in Our image, according to Our
likeness; let them have dominion over the fish of
the sea, over the birds of the air, and over the
cattle, over all the earth and over every creeping
thing that creeps on the earth." 27 So God
created man in His own image; in the image of
God He created him; male and female He created
them. 28 Then God blessed them, and said to
them, "Be fruitful and multiply; fill the earth and
subdue it; have dominion over the fish of the sea,
over the birds of the air, and over every living
thing that moves on the earth."

The word dominion means to influence, to lead,
to govern, to have power and authority.   All
through Genesis chapter one lives the heart of
God's purpose for creating mankind because the
word dominion is pregnant with the concept of

leadership. God issued the mandate of dominion to ALL humanity not just the "elect select" or certain people who may have big businesses, entourages, or even large churches. We are all called to lead in the areas of our gifting.

Notice though what God declares twice in this passage before He charges us with dominion – we are made in His image! This is a law of life. We will never take dominion in the Earth until we know the roots of our identity and assignment are in Him and not in everything else in this world. Like Jesus in John 13:3, we must KNOW we came from our Father, are going back to our Father, and that He's given all things into our hands!

Note: The word for "man" in Genesis 1:26 is not one man but rather a species, and includes male and female. He says repeatedly, let THEM have dominion over the fish, the birds, and all that creeps upon the Earth. Yet He never says take dominion over each other. This means God's original design was for male and female to co-rule together instead of competing with and trying to dominate each other. Do not fall for all the psychobabble in today's culture and media which tries to pit men and women against each other. That is clearly a result of the original sin Jesus redeemed us from!

You may say, "Well, God desired dominion and partnership, but sin entered and the fall happened." Yes, but as was pointed out in chapter three on restoration, Jesus Christ powerfully and triumphantly reconciled us to our identity, mission, and leadership again!

Who Me? Can't be!

When you first hear your real identity in Christ, you're often skeptical because who God is saying you are may not line up with your life experiences, your feelings, or your past behaviors. Just know that in battling your doubts, you're in good company!

Moses was employed by his father-in-law, thinking he was just an ordinary shepherd. Then his Creator/Manufacturer starts painting a different picture, "No Moses, you're selling yourself short. You're going to be My chosen deliverer and the leader of one million people. You're going to be the author of the first five books of the Bible and the law giver for all nations." What was Moses response? You guessed it! "God, you got the wrong guy!"

Gideon is fearful and in hiding when God finds him. His Creator says, "You are a mighty man of valor. I will save Israel by your hand." His response? "God, you can't be talking about me!" Gideon, like many of us, couldn't believe who God said he was. He's like, "God, I was born in the wrong family. I'm from the wrong part of town. I'm no mighty warrior." So he says if the fleece is wet in the morning, I'll believe. It was wet. So then he says if the fleece is dry in the morning, I'll believe. It was dry! Finally, he decides to participate with God's view of him!

We must get to the place where God's Word in us and about us matters more than anything else. We must be able to say, "I am who I am because the I AM says I am!"

When we know who we are as God's Spirit-empowered offspring, we will take exception to the enemy messing with our friends and family! We will quit praying away our Goliaths and start slaying them instead. We will quit putting up with certain doctor reports, adversities, and circumstances we were given the power and authority to change!

Imagine if we as Christians quit believing all the lies the enemy has told us. Imagine if we assigned more value to who God says we are than what we feel some times. We would see a wave of awakened and activated leadership throughout the body of Christ that would shake the world.

You need to realize as God's ambassador that God can use the opposition and adversity you face to show you who you really are. Look at David. If Goliath never showed up on that battlefield, David may have never known the true magnitude of the warrior king anointing God had placed upon his life! We must stop running from our potential and purpose, and embrace who God says we are, trusting in His power not ours.

The Lie of Lack and the Loss of Dominion

John 13:3 says, "Jesus, knowing that the Father had given all things into His hands, and that He had come from God and was going to God took off His outer garment..."

Jesus knew He had come from God, was going back to God, and all things had been given into His hands. He knew His identity, His origin, His assignment, and that He had been given authority to walk it out. This understanding and confidence manifested in amazing demonstrations where God's power and love thumped the works of the devil and the kingdom of darkness. The body of Christ however, like Jesus' first disciples, can often struggle to believe who God says we are and what we possess in Him. This "lie of lack" results in a loss of confidence and a loss of dominion as we see below.

In Matthew 17:20, Jesus said the disciples couldn't cast out certain devils because of their unbelief. Unbelief about what? I think it was unbelief about who they were, Whose authority they had, and Whose image they were made in.

Acts 19:11-16 records, "Now God worked unusual miracles by the hands of Paul, 12 so that even handkerchiefs or aprons were brought from his body to the sick, and the diseases left them and the evil spirits went out of them. 13 Then some of the itinerant Jewish exorcists took it upon themselves to call the name of the Lord Jesus over those who had evil spirits, saying, "We exorcise you by the Jesus whom Paul preaches." 14 Also there were seven sons of Sceva, a Jewish chief priest, who did so. 15 And the evil spirit answered and said, "Jesus I know, and Paul I know; but who are you?" 16 Then the man in whom the evil spirit was leaped on them, overpowered them, and prevailed against them, so that they fled out of that house naked and wounded."

Notice, "I know Jesus and I know Paul, but who are you?" We better know the answer to that question or we too will get stripped, beaten, and thrown out of the house!

When the enemy comes against your family, business, church, or city and he asks you, "Who are you?" Rise up in the authority of Christ and say, "I'm a blood bought, Spirit-filled, saint of the most High God! I'm a personal ambassador of the Lord Jesus Christ and your days of messing with my loved ones have come to an abrupt end! Here are your eviction papers; now get out!"

If you want to take dominion for Christ, if you want to advance your Father's Kingdom of righteousness, peace, and joy, if you want to break assignments levied against your family, church, business, or city, then know the truth of your identity and all you possess in Christ!

As I mentioned before, you are a joint heir with Jesus Christ. All you saw Him possess and walk in with His Father, you possess too!

Please consider this. If you are in Christ and He is in you, then when you stand against evil it is Christ Himself who is standing against evil through you!

Four Points to Remember:

- We will never take dominion until we anchor our identity in Christ not in the things of this world.
- God's Word to us and about us must carry more weight than anything else.
- We need to quit putting up with things we've been given authority to change.
- In Christ, we can quit praying away our Goliaths and start slaying them.

Chapter Seven
The Need for Emerging Leaders

America, the world, and certainly the body of Christ are all in dire need of seasoned, emerging leaders. Our communities need great role models, our children need great parents, and our world needs to see the very light and salt of Christ. We need those who not only lead like Jesus (by what He supplies not by what He demands), but also who lead with integrity. Meaning, what they say is actually one with how they live and their words are actually one with their actions.

I heard a gentleman lamenting just prior to the U.S. presidential election in 2016, "There are six billion people on the planet and these are the two best candidates the United States of America can come up with? We have a leadership deficit."

Matthew 28:18-20 says, "And Jesus came and spoke to them, saying, "All authority has been given to Me in heaven and on earth. 19 Go therefore and make disciples of all the nations, baptizing them in the name of the Father and of the Son and of the Holy Spirit, 20 teaching them

*to observe all things that I have commanded you;
and lo, I am with you always, even to the end of
the age."*

This passage in Matthew is a direct commission
to the body of Christ to provide leadership for
nations, to teach and instruct them in truth, and to
live according to the Spirit of God.

This passage combined with Ephesians 4:11-16
confirms God's plan for setting leadership in the
church in order to identify, develop, and deploy
mature believers throughout the world.
Too often though, the focus of the American
church has not been shaping the future of the
Earth but rather telling everyone about Heaven.
Instead of preparing people to *lead* the planet, the
church has focused on preparing people to *leave*
the planet!

Politically Incorrect Leaders

There are a lot of leadership styles and ideas
around, but it is quality, Spirit-filled leadership
that's one of the keys to a great turn around in the
body of Christ and the nation.

We as God's creation were designed to be subject only to Christ's Spirit, therefore, if any other spirit possesses or influences us, we are unable to function as the leaders God intended.

It is impossible for an unrighteous world, void of the Spirit of God, to produce righteous and Spirit led leaders. Thus, I conclude that Godly, qualified leaders are those who are humble, filled with and led by God's Spirit. This may sound "politically incorrect" but man has had plenty of opportunities to impress God with our wisdom; we need the wisdom and leadership of God in the days in which we live. If the church is not raising up quality leaders, then who will? The world tries but they are secularists and naturalists at best, which locks them into only man's realm for ideas. Any solutions for life on this planet will not come from this planet, but from the God who made us (and made this planet).

12 Key Thoughts on Leadership:

1) <u>We are all predestined to be conformed to the image of Jesus Christ who is the greatest leader the world has ever seen.</u>

Jesus' leadership style is not like the world. He

leads by what He supplies not by what He demands. He leads by serving not by being served. Jesus actually did ministry in front of His disciples, then with them, and then turned it over to them upon His departure. This is outstanding leadership. Jesus was making sure the dominion mandate He came to resurrect didn't die with Him. He actually equipped His disciples to carry on His mission and equip others to do the same.

There are varying types of leaders. First, there are those who want to meet everyone's need themselves so they do not invest much in developing others. Second, there are those leaders who equip and train others to do what they know how to do. They can meet the needs of those around them, but they enjoy equipping others to meet those needs. Thirdly, there are leaders like Jesus, who equip others to be able to equip others. I thank God for anyone who has a heart to help people, but obviously those who can equip others to equip others is optimum.

2) <u>According to Jesus, leadership is not about being served it's about serving.</u>

In Matthew 20:25-28 (NIV) He says, "You know that the rulers of the Gentiles lord it over them, and their high officials exercise authority over them. 26 Not so with you. Instead, whoever wants to become great among you must be your servant, 27 and whoever wants to be first must be your slave— 28 just as the Son of Man did not come to be served, but to serve, and to give his life as a ransom for many."

Great leaders never desire to lead, they actually desire to serve. We will never achieve success in transforming life on this planet by reducing people to serving us, but rather by raising up people to serve the Lord and others.

Jesus never rebuked His disciples for wanting to do great and be great, He simply tells them not to go about it the way the world does. Greatness is not how many people serve you but how many people you serve. Jesus not only taught but demonstrated that leadership doesn't come from selfish ambition and one's own desire to be great, but from a deep desire to serve and empower others. This is a great bridge to number three!

3) <u>Leadership is not about power it's about empowerment.</u>

Too many people think leadership is about having a title. Isn't it possible as God's child when you get promoted in church, business, or ministry, you weren't put "over" others but God placed you "underneath" others so you could serve, empower, and strengthen them?

How many people sit in churches week after week and think, "That speaker sure is a powerful person," when a better question is, "Do they empower others?" It's great if you are part of a body that has a leader with the gift of healing for example, but optimum leadership in the Kingdom would be that he or she activates gifts in others as well.

Recently I was at a missions conference and the theme over and over again was: We want to shift our focus from going into a city or village and just seeing people we can serve. We really want to go in with the mindset we are here to empower you to carry on Christ's mission in your town or city. We don't want to do all the work/ministry for you, we want to leave a Kingdom deposit so you can carry on the Lord's work here.

4) <u>The ultimate goal of leadership is not followers but leaders.</u>

We become the most effective leaders when those we lead can lead others.

The first time I ever heard Myles Munroe say, "The goal of leadership is not maintaining followers but developing leaders," I almost fell out of my chair. I not only thought of how much I was needing to grow in this revelation, but also my heart immediately went out to the body of Christ in America who has not seen this modeled much at all.

5) <u>Leadership is not about manipulation it's about inspiration.</u>

A quality leader not only knows where they are going, they can inspire others to go with them. They so trust the Word of the Lord in their heart and their mouth, they are able to stay clear of manipulation and leave the results to God. They also never "bulldoze" change, they "lead" change.

Leaders are comprised of authenticity, humility, integrity, and vision that inspires others toward trust and confidence. A goal as leaders should be to inspire people toward Christ and toward their true identity in Him.

6) <u>Leadership is not about doing something, it's about being who God created *you* to be.</u>

It is so important that you always remember that you are an original. You have your own set of fingerprints that no one else on the planet has! God Himself has gifted you with certain gifts and personality traits for a reason. While you can glean ideas and inspiration from other leaders, it's important you know how God has wired you to lead. Just be you as you lead because who you are becoming in Christ is more important than what you do.

As you develop daily in your true identity and call in Christ, you empower others to be the original that they are. The best thing you can do for your family and loved ones is become the person your Father created *you* to be.

7) <u>Leadership looks beyond someone's present condition to their potential.</u>

Jesus modeled this so well! If you look at His disciples, He sure didn't pick them because of their present condition. They were not exactly world changers when He called them, but by the time He and the Holy Spirit were done with them they were.

As God-breathed leaders we recognize potential in people they don't even see in themselves. This is important because many people are held back not by who they are but by who they believe they are not!

8) <u>Leaders lead with their lives not just their words.</u>

Ecclesiastes 7:1 says, "A good name is better than precious ointment."

You want a missing component in today's culture, especially among politicians and leaders? INTEGRITY! As Christians, our message is so important. We have been entrusted with the Gospel of the Kingdom of God. It is our actions and attitude that actually give value to our words, so it is imperative they are ONE with our message.

The credibility, trust, and legitimacy of leadership is rooted in integrity and sincerity. A lot of people think good leadership is rooted in talent or competency, but I beg to differ.

The Good News of Christ's Life within is so good and so beautiful, it can't just be said it must be seen! This is one of the many things that made Jesus the greatest leader the world has ever witnessed. He didn't just preach the message God so loved the world, He lived that message in deed and in creed.

As a parent, pastor, or politician, we too must lead with our lives not just our words. We cannot just talk righteousness, peace, and joy, we must live righteousness, peace, and joy. Let's be the kind of person we want others to be. We can whine and complain about other people that drive us crazy all day long, but the best thing we can do for them is BE THE PERSON we'd like them to be.

It's not our goal to match insult for insult with our culture, but to live out before the world the power of Christ's indwelling Spirit. We should daily put Jesus on display for all the world to see.

I'll never forget what the Lord said when He shared with me His desire to clean up some things in my personal life. He whispered, "Steve, I will always love you no matter what you do, but people are not that way. While the enemy can never discredit My message, he will try to discredit My messengers. Always let it be your heart's desire to live with what you preach."

9) <u>Quality leaders do not say, "What I do in private is no one's business but mine."</u>

Although we understand we are not responsible for other people's choices, we do understand our choices affect other people. As light and salt in this world, our personal decisions are never just "private" decisions. Our choices affect our spouse, friends, family, and church. They also affect people's view of the overall body of Christ, not just their view of us and our family.

Walking in integrity protects your role, resources, reputation, and relationships. All of those are huge contributors to your effectiveness as a leader and influencer for Christ. I can only imagine the number of parental rights (roles) that have been lost due to poor decisions and a lack of integrity.

As a leader, your life not only belongs to you and the Lord, but to those you are leading. Choose wisely and "include the Lord" in every decision and aspect of every day.

10) <u>Seasoned leaders understand the fruit of the Spirit is more important than the gifts of the Spirit.</u>

It is your integrity, not your gifts that will protect

you long term. So many athletes, musicians, and even ministers have stumbled because their gifts took them further than their character could keep them.

Make sure you allow the Lord and those He has placed around you for love, correction, and support to develop your character as much as your gifts. God will always prioritize the person you're becoming in Christ over what you can do for Him.

I would also caution you as a leader of a business or ministry not to simply promote people because they can "do the job." They may be incredible up front but are they the same person behind the scenes?

Quality leaders are made when a person enters into Kingdom connections (Spirit led relationships) and gets developed in their true identity, integrity, and intimacy with Jesus, not just their gifts.

11) <u>Seasoned leaders know how to measure success.</u>

I have seen so many ministries succumb to overwhelming pressure and pain because they did not understand how Jesus measures success. Because the leaders of those ministries felt pressure in chasing some carnal form of greatness, they passed the pressure onto those around them who fled or folded under the weight.

The best way to measure success in this life is to be who God says you are, do what He asks you to do, and leave the results to Him! In other words, Jesus measures success not by nickels, numbers, knowledge, or noses but by obedience.

If the Lord calls and equips you to pastor 500 people, then humbly shepherd them with all your heart. If the Lord calls and equips you to pastor 100 people, then do the same. Whatever the Lord asks you to do, you should do it with your whole heart knowing your success is being obedient to His call and His commands.

12) <u>Quality leaders seek honor from God over honor from people.</u>

Jesus told Paul in Acts 26:17, "I will deliver you from those I send you to." I believe every one of us have to be delivered from needing the approval and affirmation of those we are leading and influencing. The Lord told me on more than one occasion when I first began pastoring at Grace Church, "Steve, if you *need* them, you can't *lead* them. You should be more concerned with offending Me by not saying what I ask you to say than you are worried about offending them by saying it."

Jesus mentioned in John 12:43 how the Pharisees loved praise from men instead of the honor that comes from God. This is easy to fall into, but I encourage you to continually resist needing the affirmation of others to feel like you're valuable and significant. Those things should come from your Heavenly Father alone.

Personal Attributes of a "Spirit Led" Leader:

- Has a personal relationship and personal intimacy with the Lord every day.
- Has their confidence in God and His ability not in themselves.
- Seeks God's will not their own.
- Is grounded, authentic, and humble.
- Enjoys serving others.
- Is motivated by the love of God at all times.
- Is God-dependent not self-dependent or man-dependent.

Chapter Eight
Devoted, Developed, and Deployed

Perhaps at this point in your reading, you are
fired up enough to charge Hell with a water
pistol, but living as one of Christ's leaders and
influencers is not easy. It requires being highly
intentional and highly invested. Author Henry
Nouwen wrote, "The Spirit led life is impossible
without discipline." I pray words like, "devout,
devoted, disciplined, and dedicated" will be
words used to describe you one day if they're not
already.

The fact we are "in the Spirit" is by God's doing,
but to walk and live by His Spirit is our choice.
He alone made us His children and placed His
Spirit inside us, but only after we gave Him our
consent. Therefore, God does infuse us with His
ability (grace), but only as we give we give Him
our *availability (faith)*.

I believe with all my heart, if we will provide the
"will" God will supply the "power." If we will
daily yield to His work in our hearts, good fruit is
sure to follow. However, He will not make us
yield. His grace needs to be mixed with our faith.

Too often, churches are filled with doctrines that convince people we must either bring both the will and the power (availability and ability), resulting in self effort and burnout; or they say we need not bring anything, God does it all, resulting in indifference and apathy.

2 Corinthians 5:18-21 says, "Now all things are of God, <u>who has reconciled us to Himself through Jesus Christ, and has given us the ministry of reconciliation</u>, 19 that is, that God was in Christ reconciling the world to Himself, not imputing their trespasses to them, and has committed to us the word of reconciliation. 20 <u>Now then, we are ambassadors for Christ,</u> as though God were pleading through us: we implore you on Christ's behalf, be reconciled to God. 21 For He made Him who knew no sin to be sin for us, that we might become the righteousness of God in Him."

This is one of my favorite passages! God has reconciled us to Himself in Christ, given us the ministry of reconciling others, and named us His ambassadors! An ambassador in Webster's dictionary is defined as: A diplomatic agent of highest rank, one who represents a foreign nation or sovereign; an authorized representative or messenger on assignment.

Because of the work of Christ, you and I are authorized representatives and messengers for Christ and the Kingdom of Heaven. Our role in extending God's government will not be without its challenges though, so let us be diligent, intentional, and invested in our personal growth in Christ. Let us posture ourselves to being genuine followers of Christ who are *devoted, developed, and deployed*!

A Devoted Follower of Christ:

1) Abides in Jesus daily.

In John 15:4-5 (ESV) Jesus says, "Abide in me, and I in you. As the branch cannot bear fruit by itself, unless it abides in the vine, neither can you, unless you abide in me. 5 I am the vine; you are the branches. Whoever abides in me and I in him, he it is that bears much fruit, for apart from me you can do nothing."

Jesus' command is to abide not "go bear fruit." If you will simply abide (live, remain, stay) in Jesus daily you will bear more fruit than you ever thought possible. The Lord has told me often this past year, "Steve, if you will spend time resting in

My presence and My glory, then My presence and My glory will rest on you."

As someone who abides in Jesus daily, you understand Jesus is Lord of every day not just Lord of Sunday morning. You include Him in every choice and decision you make. He is the very love of your life, not some religious obligation. You sit with Him and learn of Him. You crave feeding your spirit man as much as feeding your physical man.

2) Knows the value of the Scriptures and their purpose in bringing you to Jesus.

John 8:31 says, "Then Jesus said to those Jews who believed Him, "If you abide in My word, you are My disciples indeed."

The Bible was not yet written when Jesus made this declaration so please recognize your need for the written Word *and* the Living Word.

Jesus said in John 5:39-40, "You search the Scriptures, for in them you think you have eternal life; and these are they which testify of Me. 40 But you are not willing to come to Me that you may have life."

Jesus reveals the purpose of the Scriptures is to bring you into and deepen your personal relationship with Him. The written Word should always illuminate you to the Living Word.

3) Knows the power of meditation.

To meditate means to think upon again and again; to consider deeply.

Philippians 4:8-9 says, "Finally, brethren, whatever things are true, whatever things are noble, whatever things are just, whatever things are pure, whatever things are lovely, whatever things are of good report, if there is any virtue and if there is anything praiseworthy—meditate on these things. 9 The things which you learned and received and heard and saw in me, these do, and the God of peace will be with you."

One of the great byproducts of meditation is peace. Peace with God, peace with yourself, and as a result – peace with others. That is what meditating on truth does, which sure beats meditating on death, despair, and doubt. Keep in mind this lasting truth: Whatever has your attention has you.

4) Knows the value of journaling.

Prayer journaling is a tremendous tool for growing and developing your intimacy with Jesus. Here are some ways you can enact this effective discipline:

- Read Scriptures the Holy Spirit leads you to and write what they say about you.
- Read Scriptures the Holy Spirit leads you to and write what the Lord speaks to you through them.
- Sit with Jesus. Be still before Him, resting in His love. Then ask Him to speak to you and write what He says.
- Obey. Whatever He reveals to you as His devoted follower, obedience from the heart is the best worship you can give Him. Don't just amen the truth and journal the truth, live the truth. After all, Jesus did say, "If you love Me, keep My commands."

5) Values prayer as a place of intimacy with God.

Each and every one of us has had our fair share of

prayer practices and ideologies, but I have found the following truths to be very helpful and effective in my journey toward intimacy:

- *The work of prayer* is to be silent and listen to the voice that says good things about you. - Henry Nouwen
- *The purpose of prayer* is relationship not religion. Prayer is not another thing we do to prove how spiritual we are.
- *The focus of prayer* is self-surrender not self-assertion. You are aligning yourself with God's will not aligning Him with yours.
- *The place of prayer* is resting in the Lord's presence wherever you are.
- *The dialogue of prayer* is two-way. You should not be the one doing most or all of the talking. The Lord said to me, "Steve, I already know you so maybe you should let Me talk, so you can know Me."

I believe if you will live as a devoted follower of Christ, the other two (Developed & Deployed) will manifest as byproducts.

A Developed Follower of Christ:

1) Is transformed by Jesus daily.

Romans 12:1-2 (TPT) says, "Beloved friends, what should be our proper response to God's marvelous mercies? <u>I encourage you to surrender yourselves to God to be his sacred, living sacrifices.</u> And live in holiness, experiencing all that delights his heart. For this becomes your genuine expression of worship. 2 Stop imitating the ideals and opinions of the culture around you, <u>but be inwardly transformed by the Holy Spirit through a total reformation of how you think.</u> This will empower you to discern God's will as you live a beautiful life, satisfying and perfect in his eyes."

2 Corinthians 3:18 adds, "But we all, with unveiled face, beholding as in a mirror the glory of the Lord, <u>are being transformed</u> into the same image from glory to glory, just as by the Spirit of the Lord."

As a developed follower of Christ, you desire each day to be transformed into the very image of Jesus! You are actively engaged in all your personal veils coming down so you can see and reflect the glory of the Lord.

You are not passive about flesh patterns and

character flaws because you understand Jesus not only has the power to forgive all your sin but also empowers you to walk in His Holiness each day. You desire Him to be Lord of your private life not just your public life.

2) Is full of conviction not excuses.

Ambassadors of Jesus are honest and have a healthy respect for God's Holiness. "If we mess up, we fess up," as Duane Sheriff says.

As a developed follower of Christ, you are involved in spiritual family for the purpose of accountability and growth. Hearing good truth on Sundays once a week won't be enough. Jesus knew large crowds could be fickle so He formed small groups with those committed to intensive, intentional, personal transformation.

3) Emphasizes hearing AND obeying.

As a developed follower of Christ, you have a heart to obey Christ as your Head, knowing your obedience changes you, not Him. Your obedience and engaging in His transformation process doesn't grow His love for you, but it does grow your love for Him.

A Deployed Follower of Christ:

1) Lives out the ministry of Jesus daily.

Luke 4:18-19 says, "The Spirit of the LORD is upon Me, because He has anointed Me to preach the gospel to the poor; He has sent Me to heal the brokenhearted, to proclaim liberty to the captives and recovery of sight to the blind, to set at liberty those who are oppressed; 19 To proclaim the acceptable year of the LORD."

The same Holy Spirit that Jesus said anointed Him for ministry here in Luke 4 is the same One that anoints you for ministry. If the Holy Spirit anointed the first body of Christ for ministry, I can assure you He desires to anoint the current body of Christ today! The Holy Spirit anoints sincerity, honesty, and truth, so keep your heart posture humble and meek.

As a deployed follower of Christ, keep in mind you are not gunning for the goal of "having a great ministry." There is one ministry on the planet and it belongs to Jesus Christ. You and I and everyone else are simply blessed to be a part of what He is doing throughout the whole Earth.

2) Is active in investing in others.

As a deployed follower of Christ, you truly see yourself involved in the Lord's work. You are active in personal, intentional investment in others in order to make disciples, develop leaders, and reproduce Christ in them.

Matthew 9:35-38 (NLT) reads, "Jesus traveled through all the towns and villages of that area, teaching in the synagogues and announcing the Good News about the Kingdom. And he healed every kind of disease and illness. 36 <u>When he saw the crowds, he had compassion on them because they were confused and helpless, like sheep without a shepherd</u>. 37 He said to his disciples, "The harvest is great, but the workers are few. 38 So pray to the Lord of the harvest; ask him to send more workers into his fields."

The appeal of Jesus in this passage is clear – with so many lost, confused, and helpless; the remedy is more shepherds! We must not leave this directive to praying, but also acting. We must not leave it to those who stand in pulpits; we must engage and not only see ourselves as shepherds but commit to raise up other shepherds!

Any individual who has no heart for people to know Christ or be developed in Christ needs to examine their own salvation. Jesus came to get us reconnected to Heaven and our Father's Spirit so we can lead and feed those who are in need of Him.

3) Ministers from God's presence

As a deployed follower of Christ, you are intentional about allowing your times in God's presence to transition into ministry and availability to help others. Ministry instead of intimacy is idolatry, whereas, ministry born FROM our intimacy with God is beautiful.

Too many times following a dynamic worship service where people encounter God's presence, they simply go home and rate it like it was a movie. They say, "Well, God was awesome today…" without asking the Lord how He might want to use what they just learned or experienced to help others.

In the book of Isaiah though, after he encounters the Lord, Isaiah is humbled, inspired, and then makes himself available for God's use. This must be the result of our God encounters and experiences!!

Isaiah 6:5-8 (KJV) says, "<u>Then said I, Woe is me! for I am undone; because I am a man of unclean lips, and I dwell in the midst of a people of unclean lips: for mine eyes have seen the King, the LORD of hosts</u>. 6 Then flew one of the seraphims unto me, having a live coal in his hand, which he had taken with the tongs from off the altar: 7 And he laid it upon my mouth, and said, Lo, this hath touched thy lips; and thine iniquity is taken away, and thy sin purged. 8 Also I heard the voice of the Lord, saying, <u>Whom shall I send, and who will go for us? Then said I, Here am I; send me.</u>"

We see this principle again in Philippians 2:1-5 where because of our deepening friendship with the Holy Spirit, Paul admonishes us to minister to and consider those around us.

Philippians 2:1-5 (TPT) reads, "Look at how much encouragement you've found in your relationship with the Anointed One! You are filled to overflowing with his comforting love. You have experienced a deepening friendship with the Holy Spirit and have felt his tender affection and mercy. 2 So I'm asking you, my friends, that you be joined together in perfect unity—with one heart, one passion, and united in one love. Walk together with one harmonious purpose and you will fill my heart with unbounded joy. 3 Be free from pride-filled opinions, for they will only harm your cherished unity. Don't allow self-promotion to hide in your hearts, but in authentic humility put others first and view others as more important than yourselves. 4 Abandon every display of selfishness. Possess a greater concern for what matters to others instead of your own interests. 5 And consider the example that Jesus, the Anointed One, has set before us. Let his mindset become your motivation."

As a deployed follower of Christ, the Lord's presence in and upon your life as well as His daily intimacy inspires you to make yourself available to Him and empowers you to be active in His Kingdom work!

<u>Closing Thoughts</u>

The best thing to do with the truth you've heard is believe it and mix faith with it. As Jesus said in John 8:32, it is our *knowing* of the truth that sets us free, not just the truth alone. Will you dare to believe that Jesus Christ had the power, love, and integrity to restore your identity, mission, and leadership in the Earth?

A good friend of mine, Roger Tutor, said, "What if God actually put His Life and power inside us? What if, as a restored human with God's Spirit back in us, we actually have the power to do miracles as Jesus the Son of Man did? After all, Jesus said, "Follow Me." He said we could do "greater works" than He did. He also said, "All things are possible to them that believe." What if all it takes to see life change on this planet is for a restored human to believe, truly believe?"

There are so many Scriptures that detail all the incredible results of Christ's divine work on your behalf. I have listed a handful below:

- Romans 8:11 says the same Spirit that raised Christ from the dead lives in you.

- Ephesians 2:19 says you are a citizen of God's Kingdom and household.
- Romans 8:16 says you are a child of God.
- Colossians 1:14 says you are forgiven.
- Romans 8:37 says you are more than a conqueror.
- 2 Corinthians 5:20 says you are Christ's ambassador.
- Revelation 1:6 says you are a priest in the Kingdom of God.
- 1 Corinthians 6:17 says you are one Spirit with Christ.
- John 17:22 says you are full of the glory of God.
- 1 Peter 1:23 says you've been born again with an incorruptible seed.
- Colossians 2:10 says you are complete and qualified in Christ.
- Colossians 1:22 says you are holy, without blame, and free of accusation in God's sight.

Knowing that *God cannot lie*, renew your mind each day to who you really are, what you really have, and you are capable of in Christ. Purpose to be God's partner in extending His goodness, health, and love to those around you.

A Final Exhortation!

I pray this book has lit a fire in your spirit that no devil in Hell or life difficulty can quench. God loves you with an unconditional love that never relents. He loves you because of who He is not because of what you do. You don't have the power or ability to make Him be unfaithful to you. According to Ephesians chapter one, He has blessed you with every spiritual blessing in the heavenly places in Christ, and from the foundations of the world He chose you to be holy and without blame in Him. God has created you to know Him, walk with Him, and extend His image and likeness in the Earth so rest, relax, receive, and start enjoying the release of His supernatural ability through your availability!!!

All Bible translations are New King James Version unless otherwise noted:

ESV – English Standard Version
KJV – King James Version
MSG – The Message
NASB – New American Standard Bible
NIV – New International Version
NLT – New Living Translation
TPT – The Passion Translation

ABOUT THE AUTHOR

At the age of 20, Steve Eden had a personal encounter with Jesus Christ while attending Northeastern State University in Tahlequah, Oklahoma. Feeling burned out and like a complete failure as a young Christian, it was in that encounter Jesus told him, "Steve, I love you because of who I am not because of what you do. So I want you to live the rest of your life from My love and not for it."

From that time on, with the Holy Spirit's guidance, Steve has been on a journey to bring himself and others out of performance based Christianity and into a vibrant, present tense, intimate relationship with his Lord, Savior, Best Friend, and Sanctifier Jesus Christ.

Made in the USA
Lexington, KY
06 November 2019